**COOKING SERIES**

COMPREHENSIVE, STEP BY STEP COOKING

Indian Dishes

BUDGET BOOKS

Food Editor: Neil Hargreaves
Cover Design: Budget Books
Prepress: Graphic Print Group

 Essential Cooking Series: Indian Dishes
First published in 2008 by Budget Books Pty Ltd
45–55 Fairchild Street
Heatherton, Victoria, 3202, Australia

10 9 8 7 6 5 4
13 12 11 10 09

Disclaimer: The nutritional information listed under each recipe does not
include the nutrient content of garnishes or any accompaniments not listed
in specific quantitites in the ingredient list. The nutritional information for
each recipe is an estimate only, and may vary depending on the brand of
ingredients used, and due to natural biological variations in the composition
of natural foods such as meat, fish, fruit and vegetables. The nutritional
information was calculated by using Foodworks dietary analysis software
(Version 3, Xyris Software Pty Ltd, Highgate Hill, Queensland, Australia) based
on the Australian food composition tables and food manufacturers' data.
Where not specified, ingredients are always analysed as average or medium,
not small or large.

ISBN: 978 1 7418 1467 5

Printed and bound in China

Contents

An introduction to Indian dishes

Cookbooks about Indian cuisine often divide the country into four food regions; however, a more refined breakdown reveals seven distinct areas, all with different food histories and different tastes. Knowledge of the different regions of India will help you understand the wide range of flavours and food in this vibrant cuisine.

NORTH INDIA

The hearty food of the north has Muslim and Moghul influences, resulting in a variety of savoury, rich lamb and goat dishes based on cooking with ghee and cream. The cuisine was further enhanced by the tandoor method of cooking, which was indigenous to the north-west frontier, now the Punjab and Pakistan. The tandoor (clay oven), which burns wood or charcoal, imparts an unparalleled smoky flavour to mildly spiced, tender meats, lake and river fish, poultry, meat and breads. Punjabi food is simple and filling, an amalgamation of the cuisines of the Greeks, Persians, Afghans, Moghuls and northern invaders.

MAHARASHTRA

The people of Maharashtra, of which Mumbai is the capital, prepare healthy food with an emphasis on rice, vegetables (as Maharashtrians are generally vegetarians), nuts and nut oils. Often vegetables are spiced with a combination of ground and roasted cumin seeds, sesame seeds, cardamom, cinnamon and coconut. Sweet and sour dishes make for tantalising eating.

GUJURATI

From Maharashtra's neighbouring state of Gujurati comes an interesting vegetarian cuisine called thali. The food is oil-free and thali restaurant waiters will refill your bowls until you are full. Thali has become an institution in India's major cities. Gujuratis are fond of relishes and pickles.

SINDHI

The Sindhis migrated to India after the 1947 partition, bringing with them a cuisine characterised by garlic, mint-flavoured chutneys, pickles and very sweet meats. Sindhi food is not necessarily vegetarian. An example is kofta tas-me. These are meatballs swathed in a sauce of onion, tomato, chilli, ginger and coriander, and sprinkled with garam masala.

PARSI

Like Christians, the Parsis have no religious dietary restrictions. Their cuisine is not overly hot, so it is a favourite with many foreigners. Traditionally, on Sunday, Parsis (most of whom live in Mumbai) add several dhals to meat, chicken and meatballs (deep fried) with caramelised brown rice.

BENGAL

Freshwater and saltwater fish, seafood and the flavour of mustard seed dominate the Bengali diet. Fish is grilled, fried or stewed. Yoghurt is offered separately and is sometimes also used in cooking. Bengalis like lightly fried fish in a sauce Westerners would regard as curry-flavoured, yet it's relatively mild. Bengalis also love sweet dishes.

SOUTH INDIA

In the south, one finds a Brahmin cuisine, distinctive because strict South Indian Brahmins will not eat tomatoes and beetroot, as they are blood-coloured nor will they eat garlic or onion. Recipes are based on tamarind, chilli, coconut, yellow lentils and rice. These, combined with a vegetable, make sambar, a staple dish eaten with rasama, a peppery, lentil-based consommé. These two dishes are the basis of the English-inspired mulligatawny, a staple dish usually eaten twice daily. Meat and seafood are enjoyed by non-vegetarians. Steamed dumplings and pancakes made from fermented ground rice and dhal have spread from Southern India throughout India.

GOA

The Christian Portuguese had a great deal of influence on the tropical state of Goa, as did the Muslims. The Portuguese use of vinegar and the sour fruits of lokum and tamarind have combined with the Christian preference for pork and a non-vegetarian Hindu taste for lamb. Seafood, fish and fruits are plentiful. Goans also perfected the vindaloo. Try the pork vindaloo recipe on page 36, or for something milder, the cashew butter chicken on page 32.

Spices, mixes and blends

masala curry paste

INGREDIENTS

3 tablespoons fresh ginger, grated
1 teaspoon ground turmeric
1 teaspoon ground cloves
1 teaspoon ground cardamom
2 cloves garlic, crushed
6 tablespoons fresh coriander, chopped
6 tablespoons fresh mint, chopped
$1/2$ cup cider vinegar
60 ml peanut oil
2 teaspoons sesame oil
makes about 1 cup

1 Place ginger, turmeric, cloves, cardamom, garlic, coriander, mint and vinegar in a blender or food processor; process until well combined.

2 Heat oils in a frying pan. Add spice mixture. Cook, stirring, until mixture boils, then remove from heat and allow to cool.

aadoo mirch spice mix

INGREDIENTS

4 tablespoons fresh ginger, grated
1 clove garlic, chopped
12 small fresh chillies, chopped
$1/2$ teaspoon salt
makes 75 g

1 Grind ginger and garlic in a blender or food processor, or use a mortar and pestle. Remove stalks from chillies and add with salt. Purée to a smooth paste, scrape into a bowl and cover tightly. Will keep for 1 week in the refrigerator.

tandoori spice mix

INGREDIENTS

1 small onion, chopped
3 cloves garlic, crushed
$2^1/2$ cm fresh ginger, finely chopped
1–2 green chillies, seeded and chopped
1 teaspoon coriander seeds
$1/2$ teaspoon cumin seeds
$1/2$ teaspoon red chilli powder
1 teaspoon paprika
$1/2$ teaspoon salt
makes 6 tablespoons

1 Grind onion, garlic, ginger, chillies and seeds together, using a pestle and mortar, or a coffee grinder kept especially for the purpose. Add chilli powder, paprika and salt and mix well.

garam masala

INGREDIENTS

2 teaspoons cardamom seeds
2 teaspoons cumin seeds
2 teaspoons coriander seeds
1 teaspoon black peppercorns
1 teaspoon whole cloves
1 cinnamon stick, broken
$1/2$ nutmeg, grated
makes 4 tablespoons

1 Heat a heavy-based frying pan over moderate heat. Add cardamom seeds, cumin seeds, coriander seeds, peppercorns, cloves and cinnamon stick. Cook, stirring, until evenly browned. Allow to cool.

2 Using a mortar and pestle, or a coffee grinder kept especially for the purpose, grind the roasted spices to a fine powder. Add nutmeg and mix well.

madras curry paste

INGREDIENTS

6 tablespoons ground coriander
4 tablespoons ground cumin
1 tablespoon freshly ground black pepper
1 tablespoon ground turmeric
1 tablespoon black mustard seeds
1 tablespoon chilli powder
4 cloves garlic, crushed
1 tablespoon fresh ginger, finely grated
$^1/_2$ cup vinegar
2 tablespoons oil
makes about $^3/_4$ cup

1 Place coriander, cumin, black pepper, turmeric, mustard seeds, chilli powder, garlic, ginger and vinegar in a food processor or blender and process to make a smooth paste. Heat oil in a frying pan over medium heat, add paste and cook, stirring constantly, for 5 minutes or until oil begins to separate from paste.

green masala curry paste

INGREDIENTS

1 teaspoon fenugreek seeds, soaked in cold water overnight
3 cloves garlic, crushed
2 tablespoons fresh ginger, grated
12 tablespoons fresh coriander, chopped
12 tablespoons fresh mint, chopped
$^1/_2$ cup vinegar
1 teaspoon Thai fish sauce
2 teaspoons ground turmeric
1 teaspoon ground cardamom
$^1/_4$ cup sesame oil
$^1/_2$ cup vegetable oil
makes about $^1/_4$ cup

1 Place soaked fenugreek seeds, garlic, ginger, coriander, mint and vinegar in a food processor or blender and process to make a smooth paste. Add fish sauce, turmeric and cardamom and process to combine.

2 Heat the sesame and vegetable oils together in a saucepan over a medium heat for 5 minutes or until hot. Stir in paste and cook, stirring constantly, for 5 minutes or until mixture boils and thickens.

vindaloo curry paste

INGREDIENTS

1 tablespoon coriander seeds
1 teaspoon cumin seeds
1 teaspoon mustard seeds
1 teaspoon ground turmeric
1 teaspoon chilli powder
$1^1/_2$ teaspoons ground ginger
pinch ground fenugreek
$1^1/_2$ teaspoons black pepper, finely ground
1 tablespoon white wine vinegar, plus extra to serve
makes about 4 tablespoons

1 Using a mortar and pestle, or a coffee grinder kept especially for the purpose, grind the whole seeds finely. Add the remaining ground spices.

2 Gradually stir in the vinegar to make a thick, smooth paste. Store in an airtight container and moisten with an additional teaspoon of vinegar just before use.

Note: Leftover pastes may be stored in sterile airtight containers in the refrigerator for 8–10 days.

Traditional dhal

INGREDIENTS

180 g brown or red lentils
3½ cups water
1 teaspoon ground turmeric
1 clove garlic, crushed
25 g ghee or clarified butter
1 medium onion, chopped
1 teaspoon garam masala
¼ teaspoon ground ginger
1 teaspoon ground coriander
½ teaspoon cayenne pepper
serves 4

PREPARATION TIME
3 minutes

COOKING TIME
36 minutes

1 Wash lentils in cold water. Place lentils, water, turmeric and garlic
   in a large saucepan and bring to simmering point. Cover and
   simmer, stirring occasionally, for 30 minutes or until lentils are
   cooked. Remove cover from pan and bring to the boil to reduce
   excess liquid.

2 Melt the ghee or butter in a large frying pan, add the onion and
   cook for 5 minutes or until onion is soft. Stir in garam masala,
   ginger, coriander and cayenne pepper and cook for 1 minute. Stir
   spice mixture into lentils and serve immediately.

NUTRITIONAL VALUE PER SERVE   FAT 5.9 G   CARBOHYDRATE 18 G   PROTEIN 10.5 G

Samosas

INGREDIENTS

500 g plain flour
1 teaspoon salt
60 g butter
¹/₂ cup water
filling
30 g butter
1 onion, finely chopped
2 cloves garlic, crushed
2 green chillies, seeded and chopped
2¹/₂ cm fresh ginger, grated
¹/₂ teaspoon ground turmeric
¹/₂ teaspoon chilli powder
370 g lean minced beef or lamb
1 teaspoon salt
2 teaspoons garam masala
   (see page 6)
juice of ¹/₂ lemon
oil for deep-frying
makes 30

1 Sift the flour and salt into a bowl. Rub in the butter, then mix in enough water to form a pliable dough. Knead for 10 minutes, then set aside.

2 To make the filling, melt butter in a frying pan. Add onion, garlic, chillies and ginger and fry for 5–7 minutes until onion is golden.

3 Stir in turmeric and chilli powder, then add the meat and salt. Fry, stirring, until meat is cooked and mixture is fairly dry. Stir in garam masala and lemon juice and cook for 5 minutes more. Remove pan from heat and allow to cool.

4 Divide the dough into 30 balls. Flatten each ball and roll out to a paper-thin circle about 10 cm in diameter. Dampen the edges of each circle with water. Fill each pastry with approximately 1 tablespoon of filling, then pinch down the edges to seal securely.

5 Deep-fry the samosas in batches in hot oil for 2–3 minutes or until golden brown. Drain on kitchen towel and serve.

PREPARATION TIME
25 minutes

COOKING TIME
10 minutes

NUTRITIONAL VALUE PER SERVE	FAT 10.3 G	CARBOHYDRATE 6.2 G	PROTEIN 3.5 G

Crunchy split peas

INGREDIENTS

85 g yellow split peas
85 g green split peas
2 teaspoons bicarbonate of soda
oil for deep-frying
½ teaspoon chilli powder
½ teaspoon ground coriander
pinch of ground cinnamon
pinch of ground cloves
1 teaspoon salt

serves 4

PREPARATION TIME
1 hour, plus 11 hours
soaking

COOKING TIME
20 minutes

1 Place the split peas in a large bowl, cover with water, stir in
   bicarbonate of soda and set aside to soak overnight.

2 Rinse the peas under cold running water and drain thoroughly.
   Set aside for at least 30 minutes, then spread out on kitchen
   towel to dry. Heat about 5 cm of oil in a frying pan and cook split
   peas in batches until golden.

3 Using a slotted spoon, remove the peas and drain on kitchen
   towel. Transfer cooked peas to a dish, sprinkle with chilli powder,
   coriander, cinnamon, cloves and salt and toss to coat.

4 Allow peas to cool and store in an airtight container.

NUTRITIONAL VALUE PER SERVE	FAT 30 G	CARBOHYDRATE 20 G	PROTEIN 10 G

Green bean salad with coriander and ginger

INGREDIENTS

700 g snake beans
2 cm fresh ginger
1 tablespoon vegetable oil
1 tablespoon sesame oil
1 teaspoon mustard seeds
2 teaspoons cumin
$\frac{1}{2}$ teaspoon turmeric
1 green chilli, finely chopped
145 ml chicken or vegetable stock
juice of 2 lemons
1 bunch coriander, washed, dried and
   chopped
salt
85 g peanuts, roasted and chopped
lemon wedges
serves 4

PREPARATION TIME
8 minutes

COOKING TIME
18 minutes

1 Trim the beans to lengths of 8 cm and discard any discoloured ends. Peel the ginger and cut into fine matchstick-sized pieces.

2 In a wok, heat the vegetable and sesame oils and when hot, add the mustard seeds. Allow to cook for a moment or two, until the seeds start popping. Add the ginger and cook for a further minute. Add cumin, turmeric and chilli and stir until fragrant: about 2 minutes.

3 Add the beans and toss in flavoured oil to coat thoroughly. Add the stock and simmer for 5–8 minutes or until the liquid has almost completely evaporated, and beans are tender.

4 Add lemon juice, coriander and salt. Stir thoroughly to combine all ingredients, then let cool. Serve garnished with roasted, chopped peanuts and lemon wedges if desired.

NUTRITIONAL VALUE PER SERVE	FAT **20** G	CARBOHYDRATE **6** G	PROTEIN **11.5** G

Chickpea salad with spinach

INGREDIENTS

1 cup dried chickpeas
1 medium onion, peeled and halved
2 small onions, peeled and diced
½ teaspoon cloves, diced
2 bay leaves
30 ml peanut or olive oil
2 cloves garlic, chopped
½ teaspoon turmeric
1 teaspoon cumin
1 teaspoon garam masala (see page 6)
1½ tablespoons tomato paste
1 red capsicum, sliced
2 medium zucchinis, sliced on the
  diagonal
salt and pepper
500 g spinach
serves 4

1 Pick over the chickpeas and remove any that are discoloured. Place all remaining chickpeas in a large saucepan and cover with cold water. Add onion halves, cloves and bay leaves and bring to boil. Simmer for 10 minutes. Remove from heat, cover and allow to steep for 2 hours. Strain the chickpeas, keeping the water.

2 Heat the oil and cook the diced onions and garlic. Add all the spices and cook them briefly. Add the chickpeas and 2 cups of the soaking water, tomato paste and the capsicum.

3 Cover and simmer gently for about 20 minutes until chickpeas soften and liquid evaporates. Add the zucchini and salt and pepper, and stir well. Remove from heat, allow to cool slightly, then fold through the spinach leaves. Cool completely and serve.

PREPARATION TIME
10 minutes plus
2 hours steeping

COOKING TIME
30 minutes

NUTRITIONAL VALUE PER SERVE	FAT **10** G	CARBOHYDRATE **24** G	PROTEIN **12** G

Cauliflower and peas in chilli sauce

INGREDIENTS

2 tablespoons oil
1 teaspoon mustard seeds
1/2 teaspoon chilli powder
pinch of asafoetida
1 cauliflower, divided into florets
125 g fresh or frozen peas (thawed)
1 potato, cut into 1 cm cubes
2 tomatoes, peeled and finely
   chopped
1/2 teaspoon turmeric
1/2 teaspoon aadoo mirch spice mix
   (see page 6)
pinch of salt
1 tablespoon coriander leaves,
   chopped
1 teaspoon molasses
400 ml water

serves 4

1 Heat the oil in a heavy-based saucepan over moderately high heat and add mustard seeds. As soon as the seeds pop, stir in chilli powder and asafoetida. Shake the pan briefly over heat, then add the cauliflower florets and peas.

2 Fry, stirring, for a few seconds, then add potato cubes, tomatoes, turmeric, aadoo mirch, salt, coriander and molasses.

3 Stir well, cover and cook for 3–4 minutes, then add the water, mixing thoroughly. Reduce heat, cover and simmer for about 30 minutes or until vegetables are tender and sauce has thickened slightly.

PREPARATION TIME
10 minutes

COOKING TIME
35 minutes

NUTRITIONAL VALUE PER SERVE   FAT 9.5 G   CARBOHYDRATE 13 G   PROTEIN 6.5 G

Vegetable korma

INGREDIENTS

2 tablespoons vegetable oil
2 tablespoons green masala curry
  paste (see page 7)
1 teaspoon chilli powder
1 tablespoon fresh ginger, finely
  grated
2 cloves garlic, crushed
1 onion, chopped
500 g cauliflower, cut into florets
200 g green beans, cut in half
3 baby eggplants, cubed
2 carrots, sliced
125 g button mushrooms
400 g canned tomatoes, mashed in
  their juices
1 cup vegetable stock
serves 4

PREPARATION TIME
10 minutes

COOKING TIME
30 minutes

1 Heat the oil in a saucepan over medium heat, stir in masala paste
   and chilli powder and cook for 2 minutes. Add the ginger, garlic
   and onion and cook, stirring, for 3 minutes or until onion is soft.
   Add the cauliflower, beans, eggplants, carrots and mushrooms
   and cook, stirring, for 5 minutes.

2 Stir in the tomatoes and stock, and bring to the boil. Reduce
   heat and simmer, stirring occasionally, for 20 minutes or until
   vegetables are tender.

NUTRITIONAL VALUE PER SERVE	FAT 14 G	CARBOHYDRATE 11 G	PROTEIN 8 G

Potato and pea bhajis

INGREDIENTS

3–4 tablespoons oil
1 onion, thinly sliced
1 teaspoon turmeric
1 teaspoon cumin seeds
¼ teaspoon ground ginger
1 green chilli, seeded and chopped
500 g potatoes, peeled and diced
250 g fresh or frozen peas (thawed if
   frozen)
fresh coriander leaves, to garnish
serves 4

PREPARATION TIME
8 minutes

COOKING TIME
30 minutes

1 Heat the oil in a flameproof casserole dish, add the onion and fry
   for 5–7 minutes, stirring frequently, until browned but not crisp.

2 Stir in turmeric, cumin seeds, ginger and chilli, then add potatoes
   and cook gently for 5 minutes, stirring frequently.

3 Stir in the peas. Cover casserole and simmer over very low heat for
   15–20 minutes, or until potatoes are tender but retain their shape.
   Garnish with coriander and serve.

NUTRITIONAL VALUE PER SERVE   FAT **16** G   CARBOHYDRATE **24** G   PROTEIN **7** G

Tandoori chicken

INGREDIENTS

2 x 1 kg fresh chickens
3 tablespoons tandoori spice mix
    (see page 6)
200 g natural yoghurt
2 tablespoons lemon juice
1 tablespoon butter, melted
lettuce leaves, onion rings, tomato
    wedges and lemon slices

serves 4–5

PREPARATION TIME
10 minutes, plus
12 hours refrigeration

COOKING TIME
1 hour

1 Rinse chickens inside and out and pat dry with kitchen towel.
   Make deep gashes in thighs and on each side of breast.

2 Mix tandoori spice mix, yoghurt, lemon juice and melted butter
   together. Place chickens in a stainless steel or non-metallic dish
   and spread mixture over, rubbing well into gashes. Cover and
   refrigerate for 12 hours.

3 Preheat the oven to 190°C. Place chickens on a roasting rack in a
   baking dish and spoon remaining marinade over them.

4 Roast for 1 hour, baste with pan juices during cooking. When
   cooked, cover with foil and rest for 10 minutes before serving.

5 Arrange crisp lettuce leaves on a large platter and cover with
   onion rings. Cut chicken into portions and place on the platter.
   Garnish with tomato wedges and lemon slices and serve
   immediately.

NUTRITIONAL VALUE PER SERVE	FAT 36.5 G	CARBOHYDRATE 3 G	PROTEIN 54 G

Roasted patiala chicken breasts

INGREDIENTS

1 medium onion, peeled and pureed
1 teaspoon salt
4 cloves garlic, chopped
2 tablespoons coriander leaves,
   chopped, plus extra leaves to
   garnish
4 cardamom pods, husks discarded
2 tablespoons natural yoghurt
$1/2$ cup butter, melted
2 tablespoons tandoori spice mix
   (see page 6)
4 skinless chicken breasts
serves 4

PREPARATION TIME
30 minutes, plus
6 hours refrigeration

COOKING TIME
25 minutes

1 Cook the onion in a small saucepan over a medium heat for
   5 minutes and cool.

2 Using a mortar and pestle, grind the salt, garlic, coriander and
   cardamom seeds to a paste. Transfer to a non-metallic bowl, stir
   in the yoghurt, butter, tandoori spice mix and onion puree, and
   mix together well.

3 Score each chicken breast 4 times with a sharp knife, and coat
   chicken thoroughly. Cover and chill for 6 hours.

4 Preheat the oven to 220°C. Place the chicken breasts on a rack in
   a roasting dish and cook for 20–25 minutes until tender and the
   juices run clear when the chicken is pierced with a skewer. Serve
   with basmati rice.

NUTRITIONAL VALUE PER SERVE   FAT 27 G   CARBOHYDRATE 25 G   PROTEIN 80 G

Kashmiri chicken

INGREDIENTS

1 onion, finely chopped
3 tablespoons fresh ginger, grated
2 cloves garlic, crushed
$1/2$ teaspoon ground coriander
$1^1/2$ teaspoons anchovy essence
1 cup ground almonds or cashews
1 tablespoon oil
4 chicken pieces, skinned
1 cup chicken stock
1 cup thick coconut milk
2 teaspoons light brown sugar
serves 4

1 Mix onion, ginger, garlic, coriander and anchovy essence with ground almonds or cashews to form a paste.

2 Heat the oil in a large heavy-based saucepan. Add the paste and stir over moderate heat for 5 minutes.

3 Add the chicken pieces and cook for 15 minutes, stirring frequently to coat in the spice mixture and seal.

4 Pour in the stock, stirring to combine with the spice mixture. Bring to the boil, reduce heat and simmer for 20 minutes.

5 Stir in the coconut milk and brown sugar, turn heat to lowest setting and simmer for 20 minutes more.

PREPARATION TIME
10 minutes

COOKING TIME
1 hour

NUTRITIONAL VALUE PER SERVE	FAT 50 G	CARBOHYDRATE 7 G	PROTEIN 30.5 G

Northern Indian chicken curry

INGREDIENTS

4 tablespoons ghee
2 cups sliced onions
2 teaspoons salt
1 teaspoon freshly ground black
  pepper
2 teaspoons sugar
1 tablespoon garlic, minced
1 tablespoon ginger, minced
2 tablespoons red chillies, minced
1 bay leaf
2 tablespoons garam masala
  (see page 6)
8 large chicken drumsticks
2 cups diced tomatoes
1 tablespoon tomato paste
serves 4

1 In a large saucepan, heat the ghee. Stir-fry the onions until glossy. Season with salt, black pepper and sugar. Continue to stir-fry until soft but do not allow to brown.

2 Add the garlic, ginger, chillies, bay leaf and garam masala. Stir-fry for 1 to 2 minutes until spices become aromatic.

3 Add the chicken pieces, tomatoes and tomato paste and cook over a medium heat for about 20 minutes, adding water a little at a time if needed. Taste and adjust seasoning with salt, pepper and sugar. Serve with Indian naan bread.

PREPARATION TIME
10 minutes

COOKING TIME
40 minutes

NUTRITIONAL VALUE PER SERVE	FAT 42 G	CARBOHYDRATE 11 G	PROTEIN 92 G

Salad of spiced chicken and dhal

INGREDIENTS

6 cups vegetable stock
1½ cups dried lentils
juice of 2 lemons
2 tablespoons vegetable oil
1 tablespoon madras curry paste
  (see page 7)
1 tablespoon garam masala
  (see page 6)
1 teaspoon turmeric
salt and pepper
4 large skinless chicken breast fillets
1½ cups vegetable stock, extra
1 small cauliflower, cut into florets
1½ cups fresh or frozen peas
  (thawed)
2 small tomatoes, seeded and diced
1 cucumber, peeled and diced
2 spring onions, sliced
2 tablespoons fresh mint, chopped
2 large bunches watercress, trimmed
fresh mint, to garnish
spring onion, to garnish
serves 4

1 Bring the vegetable stock to the boil and add the lentils. Simmer until lentils are tender: about 20 minutes. Drain well, then transfer lentils to a large bowl and add lemon juice and 1 tablespoon of oil. Mix well, cover and chill.

2 Combine the curry paste, garam masala and turmeric in a plastic bag with salt and pepper to taste, then add chicken. Seal and shake well. Heat a grill pan with the remaining oil until smoking. Add chicken to the pan and fry on both sides until golden brown and cooked through: about 5 minutes. Remove the chicken and set aside.

3 To the used pan, add the extra stock and bring to a boil. Add cauliflower and peas and cook over high heat until most of the liquid has evaporated: about 5 minutes. Add the vegetable mixture to the lentils and mix well. Add the tomatoes, cucumber, spring onions and fresh mint and mix well. Season to taste.

4 Slice chicken into strips then gently mix into salad. Arrange watercress on a platter and top with salad mixture. Garnish with fresh mint and spring onion.

PREPARATION TIME
15 minutes

COOKING TIME
35 minutes

NUTRITIONAL VALUE PER SERVE	FAT 36 G	CARBOHYDRATE 41 G	PROTEIN 110 G

Chicken biryani

INGREDIENTS

3 tablespoons ghee
3 onions, sliced
1½ kg chicken pieces
2 teaspoons fresh ginger, grated
3 cloves garlic, crushed
½ teaspoon ground cumin
½ teaspoon ground cinnamon
¼ teaspoon ground cloves
¼ teaspoon ground cardamom
¼ teaspoon ground nutmeg
½ teaspoon flour
1 cup chicken stock
½ cup natural yoghurt
½ cup cream
¼ cup cashews, chopped
rice pilau
2 tablespoons ghee
½ teaspoon ground saffron
½ teaspoon ground cardamom
1 teaspoon salt
200 g basmati rice, well washed
4 cups chicken stock
2 tablespoons sultanas
serves 4

1 Heat ghee in a large frying pan and cook onions for 2–3 minutes. Remove from pan and set aside. Add the chicken to the pan and cook until well browned on all sides. Remove and set aside.

2 Combine ginger, garlic, cumin, cinnamon, cloves, cardamom, nutmeg and flour. Stir into pan and cook for 1–2 minutes. Add stock, yoghurt and cream, and stir thoroughly.

3 Return the chicken to the pan, with half the onions. Cover and simmer for 20 minutes. Remove from heat and stand, covered, for 15 minutes. Preheat the oven to 180°C.

4 To make the rice pilau, heat the ghee in a large saucepan. Cook spices, salt and rice for 1–2 minutes. Pour in stock and bring to boil. Add sultanas, reduce heat and cook gently for 10–15 minutes. Cover and set aside for 10 minutes.

5 Transfer half the rice to a large ovenproof dish, top with chicken pieces, then with remaining rice. Drizzle over the sauce from the chicken, and top with remaining onions and cashews. Cover and bake for 20–30 minutes.

PREPARATION TIME
20 minutes

COOKING TIME
1 hour 30 minutes

NUTRITIONAL VALUE PER SERVE	FAT 59 G	CARBOHYDRATE 54 G	PROTEIN 90.5 G

Cashew butter chicken

INGREDIENTS

40 g ghee or butter
2 cloves garlic, crushed
2 small onions, finely chopped
1 tablespoon madras curry paste
  (see page 7)
1 tablespoon ground coriander
½ teaspoon ground nutmeg
550 g chicken thigh or breast fillets,
  cut into 2 cm cubes
40 g cashews, roasted and ground
1 cup double cream
2 tablespoons coconut milk
serves 4

PREPARATION TIME
10 minutes

COOKING TIME
1 hour

1 Melt ghee or butter in a saucepan over medium heat, add garlic
   and onions and cook, stirring, for 3 minutes or until onions are
   golden.

2 Stir in curry paste, coriander and nutmeg and cook for 2 minutes
   or until fragrant.

3 Add chicken and cook, stirring, for 5 minutes or until chicken is
   brown.

4 Add cashews, cream and coconut milk, bring to a boil, reduce heat
   and simmer, stirring occasionally, for 40 minutes or until chicken
   is tender.

NUTRITIONAL VALUE PER SERVE	FAT 50 G	CARBOHYDRATE 6 G	PROTEIN 30 G

Masala duck curry

INGREDIENTS

1 tablespoon sesame oil
2 kg duck, cleaned and cut into
 8 pieces
1 onion, chopped
2 small fresh red chillies, finely
 chopped
1 stalk lemongrass, finely chopped or
 1/2 teaspoon dried lemongrass,
 soaked in hot water until soft
2 tablespoons green masala
 curry paste (see page 7)
1 1/2 cups coconut milk
3 fresh or dried curry leaves
1 tablespoon lime juice
1 tablespoon brown sugar
1 tablespoon coriander leaves,
 chopped
30 g basil leaves
3 fresh green chillies, seeded
 and sliced
2 fresh red chillies, seeded and sliced
serves 4

1 Heat the oil in a deep frying pan over medium heat. Add the duck and cook, turning frequently, for 10 minutes or until brown on all sides. Remove and drain on kitchen towel.

2 Add the onion, chopped red chillies and lemongrass to pan and cook, stirring, for 3 minutes or until onion is golden. Stir in masala paste and cook for 2 minutes longer or until fragrant.

3 Stir in the coconut milk, curry leaves, lime juice and sugar and return duck to pan. Bring to boil and simmer, stirring occasionally, for 45 minutes.

4 Add coriander, basil and sliced green and red chillies and cook for 10 minutes longer, or until duck is tender.

PREPARATION TIME
20 minutes

COOKING TIME
1 hour 10 minutes

NUTRITIONAL VALUE PER SERVE	FAT 10.2 G	CARBOHYDRATE 9 G	PROTEIN 60 G

Pork vindaloo

INGREDIENTS

3 small dried red chillies
1 teaspoon cumin seeds
1½ teaspoons coriander seeds
2 cloves
4–6 black peppercorns
2½ cm cinnamon stick
2½ cm fresh ginger, grated
2 cloves garlic, chopped
3 tablespoons white vinegar
500 g lean pork, cut in 2 cm cubes
pinch of salt
water
3 tablespoons oil
2 onions, finely chopped
serves 4

1 Dry-fry the chillies, cumin seeds, coriander seeds, cloves, peppercorns and the cinnamon stick in a frying pan for a few minutes, until the mixture starts to crackle. Do not let it burn.

2 Using a mortar and pestle, or a coffee grinder kept especially for the purpose, grind the spices with ginger, garlic and vinegar to a smooth paste.

3 Place the pork in a saucepan with salt. Pour in enough water to cover meat by about 2½ cm. Bring to the boil, reduce heat and simmer for 45 minutes or until meat is tender.

4 Meanwhile, heat the oil in a large frying pan. Fry the onions for about 10 minutes, until golden. Stir in the spice paste and fry for 2 minutes more, stirring constantly.

5 Drain the meat, reserving the cooking liquid, and add it to the pan. Stir well, cover and cook for 10 minutes over moderate heat.

6 Add about 2 cups of reserved cooking liquid. Stir well, cover and cook for 15–20 minutes more. Serve immediately with rice.

PREPARATION TIME
10 minutes

COOKING TIME
50 minutes

NUTRITIONAL VALUE PER SERVE	FAT 16.5 G	CARBOHYDRATE 3 G	PROTEIN 28 G

Mustard chilli pork

INGREDIENTS

750 g pork fillets
55 g butter, melted
30 g ghee
2 tablespoons peanut oil
3 onions, chopped
1 tablespoon black mustard seeds
2 cloves garlic, crushed
2 red chillies, chopped
$\frac{1}{2}$ teaspoon ground cumin
$\frac{1}{2}$ teaspoon ground turmeric
1 tablespoon brown sugar
1 cup water
1 tablespoon lime juice
8 lime leaves

serves 4

1 Preheat the oven to 180°C. Trim the meat of all visible fat, brush with melted butter and bake in an ovenproof dish for 30 minutes.

2 Meanwhile, heat the ghee and oil in a saucepan, and cook the onions, mustard seeds, garlic and chillies for 2–3 minutes or until onions are soft.

3 Stir in cumin, turmeric, brown sugar, water, lime juice and lime leaves. Bring to the boil, then reduce heat and simmer, uncovered, for 10 minutes or until mixture reduces and thickens.

4 Transfer mixture to a food processor or blender. Process until smooth, then return to pan. Slice the pork diagonally and add to mustard mixture. Heat through gently and serve.

PREPARATION TIME
5 minutes

COOKING TIME
30 minutes

NUTRITIONAL VALUE PER SERVE	FAT 33 G	CARBOHYDRATE 8 G	PROTEIN 42.5 G

Lamb korma

INGREDIENTS

1½ kg shoulder of lamb
salt and freshly ground black pepper
2 tablespoons ghee
1 red onion, finely chopped
1 clove garlic, finely chopped
1 tablespoon green masala curry
   paste (see page 7)
¼ teaspoon ground ginger
¼ teaspoon turmeric
⅛ teaspoon cayenne pepper
2 tablespoons flour
1¼ cups chicken stock
¾ cup sultanas
145 ml yoghurt
1 tablespoon lemon juice
serves 4

1 Cut the lamb from the bone and chop into 4 cm cubes. Season with salt and pepper.

2 Heat the ghee in a large, heavy-based saucepan, add one third of the lamb and brown well on all sides. Remove and brown the remainder in 2 batches.

3 Add onion and garlic and fry until transparent. Stir in curry paste, spices and flour and cook for 1 minute. Add chicken stock, sultanas and lamb. Bring to the boil, cover and simmer gently for 1 hour or until lamb is very tender. Stir occasionally during cooking.

4 Stir in yoghurt and lemon juice and serve.

PREPARATION TIME
10 minutes

COOKING TIME
1 hour 15 minutes

NUTRITIONAL VALUE PER SERVE	FAT 27 G	CARBOHYDRATE 26 G	PROTEIN 64 G

Tandoori lamb cutlets

INGREDIENTS

8 lamb cutlets
marinade
4 tablespoons natural yoghurt
1 teaspoon fresh ginger, grated
1 clove garlic, crushed
1 tablespoon lime juice
1 teaspoon cumin
¼ teaspoon ground cardamom
¼ teaspoon chilli powder
¼ teaspoon garam masala
  (see page 6)
serves 4

PREPARATION TIME
40 minutes

COOKING TIME
8 minutes

1 Trim meat of all visible fat and set aside.

2 To make the marinade, combine the yoghurt, ginger, garlic, lime
   juice, cumin, cardamom, chilli powder and garam masala. Add
   cutlets, toss to coat and set aside to marinate for 30 minutes.

3 Remove cutlets from marinade. Grill or barbecue for 6–8 minutes,
   turning and basting with marinade frequently.

NUTRITIONAL VALUE PER SERVE	FAT 40 G	CARBOHYDRATE 1 G	PROTEIN 20 G

Lamb and spinach curry

INGREDIENTS

2 tablespoons vegetable oil
2 onions, chopped
2 cloves garlic, chopped
2½ cm fresh ginger, finely chopped
1 stick cinnamon
¼ teaspoon ground cloves
3 cardamom pods
600 g lamb, cut into cubes
1 tablespoon cumin
1 tablespoon ground coriander
4 tablespoons natural yoghurt
2 tablespoons tomato paste
1 cup beef stock
salt and freshly ground black pepper
500 g spinach, finely chopped
2 tablespoons almonds, roasted and
   flaked

serves 4

PREPARATION TIME
10 minutes

COOKING TIME
1 hour

1 Heat the oil in a flameproof casserole dish or large, heavy-based saucepan. Fry onions, garlic, ginger, cinnamon stick, cloves and cardamom pods for 5 minutes until onions and garlic are soft and spices are fragrant.

2 Add lamb and fry for 5 minutes, turning, until it begins to colour. Mix in cumin and coriander, then add the yoghurt 1 tablespoon at a time, stirring well each time.

3 Mix together the tomato paste and stock and add to the lamb. Season with salt and pepper. Bring to the boil, reduce heat, cover and simmer for 30 minutes or until lamb is tender.

4 Stir in spinach, cover and simmer for another 15 minutes or until mixture has reduced. Remove cinnamon stick and cardamom pods and mix in almonds. Serve with plain or saffron rice.

NUTRITIONAL VALUE PER SERVE	FAT 19 G	CARBOHYDRATE 6.5 G	PROTEIN 38 G

Lamb pilau with yoghurt

INGREDIENTS

500 g lean boneless leg lamb,
  cut into 2 cm cubes
6 cloves
8 black peppercorns
4 green cardamom pods
1 teaspoon cumin seeds
2¹/₂ cm stick cinnamon
1 tablespoon coriander seeds
2 small red chillies
5 cups water
2 tablespoons ghee or oil
1 onion, finely chopped
3 cm fresh ginger, grated
2 cloves garlic, crushed
500 g basmati rice, soaked for
  30 minutes in enough water
  to cover
¹/₂ teaspoon salt
lemon, to garnish
yoghurt, to serve
serves 4

1 Put lamb cubes in a saucepan. Tie cloves, peppercorns, cardamom pods, cumin seeds, cinnamon stick, coriander seeds and chillies in a muslin bag and add to pan with the water.

2 Bring to a boil, lower heat and simmer for 40 minutes. Strain, reserving lamb cubes and stock but discarding spice bag.

3 Heat ghee or oil in a large frying pan, add onion, ginger and garlic, and fry for 2 minutes, stirring frequently. Add lamb cubes, stirring to coat them in spices. Cook for 10 minutes until golden brown.

4 Meanwhile, drain the rice and transfer to a large saucepan. Pour in enough reserved stock to cover rice by about 4 cm. Add salt. Bring to a boil, reduce heat, cover and cook for 10–15 minutes or until most of the stock has been absorbed.

5 Add rice to meat mixture in pan and fork through lightly. Cover and cook over very low heat until rice is tender, adding more stock if necessary. Garnish with lemon and serve with yoghurt.

PREPARATION TIME
40 minutes

COOKING TIME
1 hour

NUTRITIONAL VALUE PER SERVE	FAT 14 G	CARBOHYDRATE 81 G	PROTEIN 30 G

Madras curry

INGREDIENTS

30 g plain flour
salt and freshly ground black pepper
500 g stewing steak, cut into 2 cm
  cubes
55 g ghee or 4 tablespoons oil
2 onions, finely chopped
1 teaspoon turmeric
1 teaspoon ground coriander
1 teaspoon cayenne pepper
$1/2$ teaspoon ground black mustard
  seeds
$1/2$ teaspoon cumin
2 cloves garlic, crushed
145 ml hot water
55 g seedless raisins
serves 4

1 Place the flour in a plastic bag and season with salt and pepper. Add cubes of stewing steak, close bag and shake until evenly coated.

2 Heat ghee or oil in a heavy-based pan, add floured beef cubes and fry for 5 minutes, stirring and turning meat so that all sides are browned.

3 Add onions and cook, stirring occasionally, for 5 minutes longer.

4 Stir in spices and cook for 3 minutes, then add garlic. Cook for 2 minutes.

5 Add the hot water. Bring to a boil and boil briskly, stirring constantly, for 5 minutes.

6 Stir in the raisins and add more water, if necessary, to cover meat. Bring to the boil, reduce heat and simmer for $2^1/4$ hours, adding more water as required. Serve at once or cool swiftly, refrigerate and reheat next day.

PREPARATION TIME
6 minutes

COOKING TIME
2 hours 35 minutes

NUTRITIONAL VALUE PER SERVE	FAT 20 G	CARBOHYDRATE 18 G	PROTEIN 28 G

Meatballs in tomato sauce

INGREDIENTS

500 g minced lamb
5 tablespoons natural yoghurt
5 cm fresh ginger, finely chopped
1 green chilli, deseeded and finely
  chopped
3 tablespoons coriander leaves,
  chopped
2 teaspoons cumin
2 teaspoons ground coriander
salt and black pepper
2 tablespoons vegetable oil
1 onion, chopped
2 cloves garlic, chopped
$\frac{1}{2}$ teaspoon turmeric
1 teaspoon garam masala
  (see page 6)
1 tablespoon water
400 g can chopped tomatoes
150 ml water
serves 4

PREPARATION TIME
20 minutes

COOKING TIME
50 minutes

1 Mix the lamb, 1 tablespoon of yoghurt, ginger, chilli, 2 tablespoons of coriander leaves, cumin, ground coriander and salt and pepper. Shape the mixture into 16 meatballs.

2 Heat 1 tablespoon of oil in a large saucepan, then fry meatballs for 10 minutes, turning until browned. You may have to cook them in batches. Drain on kitchen towel and set aside.

3 Heat the remaining oil in the pan. Add onion and garlic and fry for 5 minutes or until softened, stirring occasionally. Mix turmeric and garam masala with water, then add to onion and garlic. Add remaining yoghurt, 1 tablespoon at a time.

4 Add tomatoes, meatballs and 150 ml of water to mixture, and bring to a boil. Partly cover the pan, reduce heat and simmer for 30 minutes, stirring occasionally. Sprinkle rest of the coriander leaves over to garnish and serve with rice.

| NUTRITIONAL VALUE PER SERVE | FAT 22.5 G | CARBOHYDRATE 6 G | PROTEIN 28 G |

Tikka skewers

INGREDIENTS

550 g firm white fish fillets,
cut into 2 cm wide strips
spicy yoghurt marinade
1 small onion, chopped
3 cloves garlic, crushed
2 teaspoons fresh ginger, grated
1 tablespoon cumin
1 tablespoon garam masala
(see page 6)
2 cardamom pods, crushed
1 teaspoon turmeric
1 teaspoon chilli powder
2 teaspoons ground coriander
$1/2$ tablespoon tomato paste
$1^1/4$ cups natural yoghurt

serves 4

1 Pierce fish strips several times with a fork and place in a shallow glass or ceramic dish.

2 To make the marinade, place onion, garlic, ginger, cumin, garam masala, cardamom, turmeric, chilli powder, coriander and tomato paste in a food processor or blender and process until smooth. Add yoghurt and mix together. Spoon marinade over fish, toss to combine, cover and marinate in refrigerator for 3 hours.

3 Preheat a barbecue to medium heat. Drain fish and thread onto lightly oiled skewers. Place skewers on lightly oiled barbecue and cook, turning several times, for 5–6 minutes or until fish is cooked. Serve skewers with lemon wedges.

PREPARATION TIME
30 minutes plus
3 hours refrigeration

COOKING TIME
6 minutes

| NUTRITIONAL VALUE PER SERVE | FAT 7 G | CARBOHYDRATE 8 G | PROTEIN 32 G |

Goan-style fish and coconut curry

INGREDIENTS

2 tomatoes
2 cardamom pods, husks discarded
  and seeds reserved
1 teaspoon each of ground coriander,
  cumin, cinnamon and chilli powder
$^1/_2$ teaspoon turmeric
2 tablespoons water
2 tablespoons vegetable oil
1 onion, finely chopped
1 clove garlic, finely chopped
$2^1/_2$ cm fresh ginger, finely chopped
400 ml coconut milk
680 g firm white fish fillet, cut into
  $2^1/_2$ cm chunks
salt
coriander leaves, to garnish

serves 4

1 Place tomatoes in a bowl, cover with boiling water and leave to stand for 30 seconds. Peel, then finely dice flesh.

2 Crush cardamom seeds. Add coriander, cumin, cinnamon, chilli powder, turmeric and water and mix to a paste. Set aside.

3 Heat oil in a large, heavy-based saucepan. Fry onion, garlic and ginger for 3 minutes or until softened. Add spice paste, mix well and fry for 1 minute, stirring constantly.

4 Pour in coconut milk and bring to the boil, stirring. Reduce heat and simmer for 10 minutes. Add fish, tomatoes and salt. Partly cover pan and simmer, stirring occasionally, for a further 10 minutes. Garnish with coriander and serve with rice.

PREPARATION TIME
15 minutes

COOKING TIME
25 minutes

NUTRITIONAL VALUE PER SERVE	FAT 31.5 G	CARBOHYDRATE 7 G	PROTEIN 43 G

Baked fish

INGREDIENTS

2 large onions, chopped
1 tablespoon vegetable oil
2 cloves garlic, crushed
2 fresh red or green chillies,
  finely chopped
2 teaspoons fresh ginger,
  finely chopped
1 tablespoon cumin seeds
2 bay leaves
salt
4 large tomatoes, finely chopped
1/2 teaspoon ground cumin
1/2 teaspoon ground coriander
pinch ground cloves
pinch ground cinnamon
pinch ground cardamom
1/2 teaspoon mango powder
1/4 teaspoon turmeric
3 tablespoons double cream
4 firm white fish fillets
1 bunch basil, finely chopped
serves 4

1 Preheat the oven to 180°C. Place onions in a food processor or blender and process to make a purée.

2 Heat oil in a heavy-based saucepan, add garlic, chillies, ginger, cumin seeds, bay leaves, salt and onion purée. Cook over a medium heat until onions are a pinkish colour. Add tomatoes, ground cumin, coriander, cloves, cinnamon, cardamom, mango powder and turmeric and cook, stirring, for 3–4 minutes. Remove pan from heat and stir in cream.

3 Place the fish in a baking dish, pour the sauce over and bake for 20 minutes or until fish flakes when tested with a fork. Garnish with fresh basil.

PREPARATION TIME
15 minutes

COOKING TIME
25 minutes

NUTRITIONAL VALUE PER SERVE	FAT 14 G	CARBOHYDRATE 10 G	PROTEIN 31 G

Chilli sesame prawn kebabs

INGREDIENTS

1 tablespoon vegetable oil
1 tablespoon madras curry paste
  (see page 7)
2 tablespoons fresh ginger, finely
  grated
2 cloves garlic, crushed
2 tablespoons lime juice
$\frac{1}{2}$ cup natural yoghurt
24 uncooked medium prawns,
  shelled and deveined, tails left on
4 tablespoons sesame seeds, toasted
green masala onions
20 g ghee or butter
2 small onions, cut into wedges
2 tablespoons green masala
  curry paste (see page 7)
serves 4

PREPARATION TIME
20 minutes, plus
2 hours refrigeration

COOKING TIME
10 minutes

1 Place oil, madras curry paste, ginger, garlic, lime juice and yoghurt
   in a bowl and mix together. Add prawns and toss to coat. Cover
   and marinate in the refrigerator for 2 hours.

2 Drain prawns and thread 3 prawns onto an oiled skewer. Repeat
   with remaining prawns to make 8 kebabs. Toss kebabs in sesame
   seeds and cook on a lightly oiled, medium barbecue or under a
   grill for 3 minutes on each side or until prawns are cooked.

3 To make masala onions, melt ghee or butter in a saucepan over a
   medium heat. Add onions and cook, stirring, for 5 minutes or until
   soft. Stir in masala paste and cook for 2 minutes or until heated
   through. Serve with the kebabs.

NUTRITIONAL VALUE PER SERVE	FAT 19.5 G	CARBOHYDRATE 3 G	PROTEIN 28 G

Spicy red prawns

INGREDIENTS

6 cloves garlic, finely chopped
2 teaspoons fresh ginger, finely
  chopped
8 fresh red or green chillies, finely
  chopped
3 tablespoons lemon juice
1 tablespoon caster sugar
salt
16 large uncooked prawns, shelled
  and deveined
3 large tomatoes, peeled, seeded and
  chopped
1 tablespoon vegetable oil
1 small bunch coriander, chopped
serves 4

PREPARATION TIME
15 minutes, plus
24 hours refrigeration

COOKING TIME
35 minutes

1 Place garlic, ginger, chillies, lemon juice, caster sugar and salt in a bowl
   and mix to combine. Add prawns and toss to coat. Cover and marinate in
   refrigerator for 24 hours.

2 Preheat the oven to 160°C. Place tomatoes in a food processor or blender and
   process until smooth.

3 Heat the oil in a wok or large frying pan, reduce heat and add prawns with
   marinade and cook, stirring constantly, for 2–3 minutes.

4 Transfer all to a casserole dish, add the tomatoes and coriander, then mix
   well to combine.

5 Cover and bake for 30 minutes.

NUTRITIONAL VALUE PER SERVE	FAT 5.5 G	CARBOHYDRATE 8 G	PROTEIN 17.5 G

Glossary

Al dente: Italian term to describe pasta and rice that are cooked until tender but still firm to the bite.

Asafoetida: a herbaceous perennial plant native to Iran. The dried sap is used as a spice. It resembles onion and garlic in flavour.

Bake blind: to bake pastry cases without their fillings. Line the raw pastry case with greaseproof paper and fill with raw rice or dried beans to prevent collapsed sides and puffed base. Remove paper and fill 5 minutes before completion of cooking time.

Baste: to spoon hot cooking liquid over food at intervals during cooking to moisten and flavour it.

Beat: to make a mixture smooth with rapid and regular motions using a spatula, wire whisk or electric mixer; to make a mixture light and smooth by enclosing air.

Beurre manié: equal quantities of butter and flour mixed together to a smooth paste and stirred bit by bit into a soup, stew or sauce while on the heat to thicken. Stop adding when desired thickness results.

Bind: to add egg or a thick sauce to hold ingredients together when cooked.

Blanch: to plunge some foods into boiling water for less than a minute and immediately plunge into iced water. This is to brighten the colour of some vegetables; to remove skin from tomatoes and nuts.

Blend: to mix 2 or more ingredients thoroughly together; do not confuse with blending in an electric blender.

Boil: to cook in a liquid brought to boiling point and kept there.

Boiling point: when bubbles rise continually and break over the entire surface of the liquid, reaching a temperature of 100°C (212°F). In some cases food is held at this high temperature for a few seconds then heat is turned to low for slower cooking. See simmer.

Bouquet garni: a bundle of several herbs tied together with string for easy removal, placed into pots of stock, soups and stews for flavour. A few sprigs of fresh thyme, parsley and bay leaf are used. Can be purchased in sachet form for convenience.

Caramelise: to heat sugar in a heavy-based pan until it liquefies and develops a caramel colour. Vegetables such as blanched carrots and sautéed onions may be sprinkled with sugar and caramelised.

Chill: to place in the refrigerator or stir over ice until cold.

Clarify: to make a liquid clear by removing sediments and impurities. To melt fat and remove any sediment.

Coat: to dust or roll food items in flour to cover the surface before the food is cooked. Also, to coat in flour, egg and breadcrumbs.

Cool: to stand at room temperature until some or all heat is removed, e.g. cool a little, cool completely.

Cream: to make creamy and fluffy by working the mixture with the back of a wooden spoon, usually refers to creaming butter and sugar or margarine. May also be creamed with an electric mixer.

Croutons: small cubes of bread, toasted or fried, used as an addition to salads or as a garnish to soups and stews.

Crudite: raw vegetable sticks served with a dipping sauce.

Crumb: to coat foods in flour, egg and breadcrumbs to form a protective coating for foods which are fried. Also adds flavour, texture and enhances appearance.

Cube: to cut into small pieces with six even sides, e.g. cubes of meat.

Cut in: to combine fat and flour using 2 knives scissor fashion or with a pastry blender, to make pastry.

Deglaze: to dissolve dried out cooking juices left on the base and sides of a roasting dish or frying pan. Add a little water, wine or stock, scrape and stir over heat until dissolved. Resulting liquid is used to make a flavoursome gravy or added to a sauce or casserole.

Degrease: to skim fat from the surface of cooking liquids, e.g. stocks, soups, casseroles.

Dice: to cut into small cubes.

Dredge: to heavily coat with icing sugar, sugar, flour or cornflour.

Dressing: a mixture added to completed dishes to add moisture and flavour, e.g. salads, cooked vegetables.

Drizzle: to pour in a fine thread-like stream moving over a surface.

Egg wash: beaten egg with milk or water used to brush over pastry, bread dough or biscuits to give a sheen and golden brown colour.

Essence: a strong flavouring liquid, usually made by distillation. Only a few drops are needed to flavour.

Fillet: a piece of prime meat, fish or poultry which is boneless or has all bones removed.

Flake: to separate cooked fish into flakes, removing any bones and skin, using 2 forks.

Flame: to ignite warmed alcohol over food or to pour into a pan with food, ignite then serve.

Flute: to make decorative indentations around the pastry rim before baking.

Fold in: combining of a light, whisked or creamed mixture with other ingredients. Add a portion of the other ingredients at a time and mix using a gentle circular motion, over and under the mixture so that air will not be lost. Use a silver spoon or spatula.

Glaze: to brush or coat food with a liquid that will give the finished product a glossy appearance, and on baked products, a golden brown colour.

Grease: to rub the surface of a metal or heatproof dish with oil or fat, to prevent the food from sticking.

Herbed butter: softened butter mixed with finely chopped fresh herbs and re-chilled. Used to serve on grilled meats and fish.

Hors d'oeuvre: small savoury foods served as an appetiser, popularly known today as 'finger food'.

Infuse: to steep foods in a liquid until the liquid absorbs their flavour.

Joint: to cut poultry and game into serving pieces by dividing at the joint.

Julienne: to cut some food, e.g. vegetables and processed meats, into fine strips the length of matchsticks. Used for inclusion in salads or as a garnish to cooked dishes.

Knead: to work a yeast dough in a pressing, stretching and folding motion with the heel of the hand until smooth and elastic to develop the gluten strands. Non-yeast doughs should be lightly and quickly handled as gluten development is not desired.

Line: to cover the inside of a baking tin with paper for the easy removal of the cooked product from the baking tin.

Macerate: to stand fruit in a syrup, liqueur or spirit to give added flavour.

Marinade: a flavoured liquid, into which food is placed for some time to give it flavour and to tenderise. Marinades include an acid ingredient such as vinegar or wine, oil and seasonings.

Mask: to evenly cover cooked food portions with a sauce, mayonnaise or savoury jelly.

Pan-fry: to fry foods in a small amount of fat or oil, sufficient to coat the base of the pan.

Parboil: to boil until partially cooked. The food is then finished by some other method.

Pare: to peel the skin from vegetables and fruit. Peel is the popular term but pare is the name given to the knife used; paring knife.

Pit: to remove stones or seeds from olives, cherries, dates.

Pith: the white lining between the rind and flesh of oranges, grapefruit and lemons.

Pitted: the olives, cherries, dates etc. with the stone removed, e.g. purchase pitted dates.

Poach: to simmer gently in enough hot liquid to almost cover the food so shape will be retained.

Pound: to flatten meats with a meat mallet; to reduce to a paste or small particles with a mortar and pestle.

Simmer: to cook in liquid just below boiling point at about 96°C (205°F) with small bubbles rising gently to the surface.

Skim: to remove fat or froth from the surface of simmering food.

Stock: the liquid produced when meat, poultry, fish or vegetables have been simmered in water to extract the flavour. Used as a base for soups, sauces, casseroles etc. Convenience stock products are available.

Sweat: to cook sliced onions or vegetables, in a small amount of butter in a covered pan over low heat, to soften them and release flavour without colouring.

Conversions

Measurements differ from country to country, so it's important to understand what the differences are. This Measurements Guide gives you simple 'at-a-glance' information for using the recipes in this book, wherever you may be.

Cooking is not an exact science – minor variations in measurements won't make a difference to your cooking.

EQUIPMENT

There is a difference in the size of measuring cups used internationally, but the difference is minimal (only 2–3 teaspoons). We use the Australian standard metric measurements in our recipes:

1 teaspoon ....5 ml   1 tablespoon....20 ml
1/2 cup......125 ml   1 cup.....250 ml
4 cups...1 litre

Measuring cups come in sets of one cup (250 ml), 1/2 cup (125 ml), 1/3 cup (80 ml) and 1/4 cup (60 ml). Use these for measuring liquids and certain dry ingredients.

Measuring spoons come in a set of four and should be used for measuring dry and liquid ingredients.

When using cup or spoon measures always make them level (unless the recipe indicates otherwise).

DRY VERSUS WET INGREDIENTS

While this system of measures is consistent for liquids, it's more difficult to quantify dry ingredients. For instance, one level cup equals: 200 g of brown sugar; 210 g of caster sugar; and 110 g of icing sugar.

When measuring dry ingredients such as flour, don't push the flour down or shake it into the cup. It is best just to spoon the flour in until it reaches the desired amount. When measuring liquids use a clear vessel indicating metric levels.

Always use medium eggs (55–60 g) when eggs are required in a recipe.

OVEN

Your oven should always be at the right temperature before placing the food in it to be cooked. Note that if your oven doesn't have a fan you may need to cook food for a little longer.

MICROWAVE

It is difficult to give an exact cooking time for microwave cooking. It is best to watch what you are cooking closely to monitor its progress.

STANDING TIME

Many foods continue to cook when you take them out of the oven or microwave. If a recipe states that the food needs to 'stand' after cooking, be sure not to overcook the dish.

CAN SIZES

The can sizes available in your supermarket or grocery store may not be the same as specified in the recipe. Don't worry if there is a small variation in size – it's unlikely to make a difference to the end result.

dry		liquids	
metric (grams)	imperial (ounces)	metric (millilitres)	imperial (fluid ounces)
		30 ml	1 fl oz
30 g	1 oz	60 ml	2 fl oz
60 g	2 oz	90 ml	3 fl oz
90 g	3 oz	100 ml	3 1/2 fl oz
100 g	3 1/2 oz	125 ml	4 fl oz
125 g	4 oz	150 ml	5 fl oz
150 g	5 oz	190 ml	6 fl oz
185 g	6 oz	250 ml	8 fl oz
200 g	7 oz	300 ml	10 fl oz
250 g	8 oz	500 ml	16 fl oz
280 g	9 oz	600 ml	20 fl oz (1 pint)*
315 g	10 oz	1000 ml (1 litre)	32 fl oz
330 g	11 oz		
370 g	12 oz		
400 g	13 oz		
440 g	14 oz		
470 g	15 oz		
500 g	16 oz (1 lb)		
750 g	24 oz (1 1/2 lb)		
1000 g (1 kg)	32 oz (2 lb)		*Note: an American pint is 16 fl oz.

cooking temperatures	°C (celsius)	°F (fahrenheit)	gas mark
very slow	120	250	1/2
slow	150	300	2
moderately slow	160	315	2–3
moderate	180	350	4
moderate hot	190	375	5
	200	400	6
hot	220	425	7
very hot	230	450	8
	240	475	9
	250	500	10

Index